The Official

LEEDS UNITED®
Annual 2016

Written by Ryan Parrish
Designed by Jon Dalrymple

A Grange Publication

© 2015. Published by Grange Communications Ltd., Edinburgh, under licence from Leeds United Football Club. Printed in the EU.

Photographs © Varley Picture Agency

ISBN 9781910199640

Welcome

Welcome to The Official Leeds United FC Annual 2016!

Despite not quite finishing where we had hoped in the Championship last time around, 2014/15 certainly brought some memorable moments and reasons for optimism at Elland Road. It was the season that saw the likes of Lewis Cook, Charlie Taylor and Kalvin Phillips make their breakthrough and combine with fellow Academy graduates Sam Byram and Alex Mowatt to give the team an exciting, home-grown core.

In this year's Annual we'll be taking a closer look at Thorp Arch's prolific production line of talent and profiling some of the gifted youngsters who could be next to make their mark at the club.

We also welcome Uwe Rosler to Leeds and get to know the Head Coach who has vowed to bring a German-influenced style of football to LS11. Uwe's impressive career is profiled within these pages, plus we'll get to meet some of his key backroom staff behind the scenes at the training ground.

Once you've delved deeper into the world of Leeds United, we have a number of quizzes and puzzles to put your knowledge to the test on all things white, yellow and blue. We hope you enjoy it.

Marching on Together!

Contents

Roll of Honour

FOOTBALL LEAGUE

1968-69 First Division Champions
1973-74 First Division Champions
1991-92 First Division Champions
1923-24 Second Division Champions
1963-64 Second Division Champions
1989-90 Second Division Champions
1927-28 Second Division Runners-up
1931-32 Second Division Runners-up
1955-56 Second Division Runners-up
2009-10 League One Runners-up

FA CUP

1972 FA Cup Winners
1965 FA Cup Finalists
1970 FA Cup Finalists
1973 FA Cup Finalists

FOOTBALL LEAGUE CUP

1968 Football League Cup Winners
1996 Football League Cup Finalists

CHARITY SHIELD

1969 FA Charity Shield Winners
1974 FA Charity Shield Runners-up
1992 FA Charity Shield Winners

FA YOUTH CUP

1993 FA Youth Cup Winners
1997 FA Youth Cup Winners

EUROPEAN \CUP

1974-75 European Cup Finalists

EUROPEAN CUP WINNERS' CUP

1972-73 European Cup-Winners' Cup Finalists

INTER CITIES FAIRS CUP/UEFA CUP

1967-68 European Fairs Cup Winners
1970-71 European Fairs Cup Winners
1966-67 European Fairs Cup Finalists

Highlights of 2014/15

Accrington Stanley (h), Capital One Cup 12.08.2014 2–1 Win

A 2-0 defeat at Millwall on the opening day wasn't the best of starts to the new season, but Leeds got off the mark in the League Cup three days later with a narrow win over League Two side Accrington Stanley. Souleymane Doukara's impressive double inside the opening 45 minutes, his first goals since joining the club, meant David Hockaday's side looked on course for a comfortable win. However, James Gray pulled one back for the visitors and Gaetano Berardi was shown a straight red card on his debut, meaning it was a nervy finale as Leeds held on to book a trip to Bradford in the next round.

Middlesbrough (h), Championship 16.08.2014 1–0 Win

Elland Road's first game of the season proved to be one of 2014/15's most dramatic as debutant Billy Sharp grabbed a late winner in front of the Sky Sports cameras. It was an end-to-end contest played in front of a lively home crowd but, after Boro's Albert Adomah had a goal ruled out and Sharp missed a clear-cut chance late on, the game appeared destined to end goalless. That was until two minutes from time when visiting goalkeeper Tomas Mejias pushed Michael Tonge's strike into the path of Sharp, who calmly tucked the ball away in front of an ecstatic Kop.

Bolton (h), Championship 30.08.2014 1–0 Win

Following the exit of Hockaday earlier in the week, Neil Redfearn stepped up to take charge for the visit of Bolton. On a glorious August afternoon at Elland Road, Stephen Warnock's 17th-minute effort proved to be the difference between the two sides, with the full-back slotting what first looked to be a cross into the bottom corner. Bolton piled on the pressure after the break but they found goalkeeper Marco Silvestri in inspired form between the sticks and were unable to pull themselves level as Leeds secured their second Championship win.

Bournemouth (a), Championship – 16.09.2014 3-1 Win

The first away win of the campaign proved to be well worth waiting for on an unforgettable night at Bournemouth's Goldsands Stadium. The hosts took an early lead through Andrew Surman, firing in after just six minutes, and could have gone even further ahead if it wasn't for the heroics of Silvestri. Doukara levelled on 69 minutes with a tidy finish into the bottom corner, before the last 10 minutes sent the travelling Leeds fans into dreamland as Giuseppe Bellusci fired in an unstoppable free-kick and Mirco Antenucci raced free to wrap things up.

Huddersfield (h), Championship 20.09.2014 3-0 Win

Things continued to get better for Redfearn's side and an emphatic 3-0 win over Yorkshire rivals Huddersfield saw United claim their first back-to-back league victories of the season. In front of 29,131 supporters at Elland Road it was a convincing display from the off, and the scoring was opened through Rodolph Austin's 20th-minute rocket. Antenucci then doubled the advantage on the stroke of half-time following a flowing counter-attack with Bellusci, before Doukara added a third midway through the second half with a powerful, low effort. However, it proved to be Redfearn's last game in the dug-out for the time being as Darko Milanic was appointed as the club's new Head Coach the following week.

Blackpool (h), Championship 08.11.2014 3-1 Win

Leeds had gone eight games without a win since the victory over Huddersfield and Redfearn was back in charge, this time on a permanent basis, following Milanic's quick exit after just six games. The visit of struggling Blackpool brought one of the finest first-half displays Elland Road had seen for some time, as goals from Liam Cooper, Doukara and Antenucci put Redfearn's men in cruise control going into the break. Nile Ranger hit back after the restart, with the visitors threatening to put up a fight, but this was a job well done heading into the final international break of 2014.

Season Review

Highlights of 2014/15

Derby County (h), Championship 29.11.2014 2-0 Win

Steve McClaren's Derby arrived at Elland Road as the league leaders but left nursing their wounds after falling to Redfearn's impressive Leeds. Antenucci was the hero on the day, scoring either side of half-time with composed finishes at each end to continue his rich vein of form in front of goal. The scoreline could have been more and the game itself proved to be one of the season's highlights, but the Leeds fans needed to savour it as they would not taste victory for another eight matches and the following week's 4-1 loss at Ipswich brought everybody back down to earth.

Nottingham Forest (a), Championship 20.12.2014 1-1 Draw

On a whole, last season's Christmas period was a forgettable one, but five days before the turkey and tinsel, Leeds claimed a respectable point from a tough 1-1 draw away to Nottingham Forest. Matty Fryatt, who also had two efforts ruled out, opened the scoring in first-half stoppage time at the City Ground as Forest enjoyed the better of the chances. But, after Sam Byram was hauled down inside the area by Danny Fox, Sharp hammered home a 54th-minute equaliser from the penalty spot to level proceedings in front of the Sky cameras.

Bournemouth (h), Championship 20.01.2015 1-0 Win

Performances were starting to look up again since the turn of the year and Leeds ended a run of eight winless games with a 1-0 victory over high-flying Bournemouth. It came in dramatic fashion, too, after Luke Murphy's stunning left-footed strike had whistled into the top corner to break the deadlock on 36 minutes. The Cherries piled on the pressure in the second half and were awarded a golden chance to equalise late on when Bellusci was shown a straight red for fouling Callum Wilson inside the area. But Yann Kermorgant smashed the bar with the resulting penalty, as United did the double over the eventual champions.

Huddersfield (a), Championship
31.01.2015   2-1 Win

Facing Huddersfield used to be something that Leeds fans dreaded but they made it three wins on the bounce over the Terriers by securing another seasonal double at the end of January. Byram had got Redfearn's men off to the ideal start with a clever finish on the turn after just seven minutes, but Harry Bunn hit back 20 minutes later to level things up. There were nervy moments aplenty for both sides in the second half as neither seemed quite sure whether to stick or twist, until Sharp arrived at the back post with a brave, last-minute header to ensure all three points would be going back to Elland Road.

Reading (a), Championship
10.02.2015 2-0 Win

Another eye-catching win came in the shape of a 2-0 victory at Reading's Madejski Stadium, courtesy of goals from in-form duo Murphy and Byram. It took 63 minutes for the net to be found, with Murphy's long-range effort proving to be too powerful for goalkeeper Adam Federici diving down to his right. Byram then added his second of the season in stoppage time after a quick breakaway, nodding in at the back post after being teed up perfectly by Steve Morison, before celebrating with the travelling army.

Millwall (h), Championship
14.02.2015 1-0 win

Just a day after his birthday, homegrown midfielder Alex Mowatt celebrated turning 20 in style by hitting the free-kick that sunk Millwall at Elland Road. His 39th-minute effort, which was helped on its way by the slightest of deflections off the visitors' wall, proved to be the difference as United's mini revival continued. It meant that Leeds had lost just once in their last seven games and any lingering fears of relegation were soon starting to ease after further back-to-back wins. The game also kick-started a fine run of form in front of goal for Mowatt.

Season Review

Highlights of 2014/15

Middlesbrough (a), Championship 21.02.2015 1-0 Win

A televised lunchtime trip to promotion-chasing Middlesbrough was next up for Redfearn's confident United side, and one of the defensive performances of the campaign helped produce another three points. It took just three minutes for Mowatt to find the bottom corner and open the scoring at the Riverside, but from there Leeds mainly found themselves camped inside their own half as the hosts threw men forward. Some goalkeeping heroics from Silvestri, who went on to claim the Man of the Match award, combined with some crucial last-gasp blocks from the likes of Sol Bamba and Bellusci, preserved the clean sheet for another memorable away win.

Ipswich (h), Championship 04.03.2015 2-1 Win

Following defeats to Brighton and Watford, Leeds got back to winning ways when play-off hopefuls Ipswich Town visited Elland Road. It had been somewhat of a non-event until 20 minutes from time, but the game burst into life when Mowatt curled home an inch-perfect free-kick in front of the Kop. Freddie Sears hit back for Ipswich, equalising within just three minutes of going behind, but Sharp made it two in two games as he fired Lewis Cook's cross into the bottom corner three minutes later. Late drama was still to come after Bamba was adjudged to have handled the ball inside the area, but Silvestri tipped Daryl Murphy's penalty onto the post to secure the three points.

Wigan (a), Championship 07.03.2015 1-0 Win

Leeds were back in the swing of things and the wins kept on coming as Wigan were the latest team to suffer defeat at the hands of Redfearn's side. On a worn and bobbly DW Stadium pitch, this was never going to be a classic, but the Mowatt strike that proved to be the difference was worthy of winning any game. The second half was just six minutes old when the ball rolled into his path, and the young midfielder hammered home an unstoppable right-footed effort beyond former United goalkeeper Scott Carson.

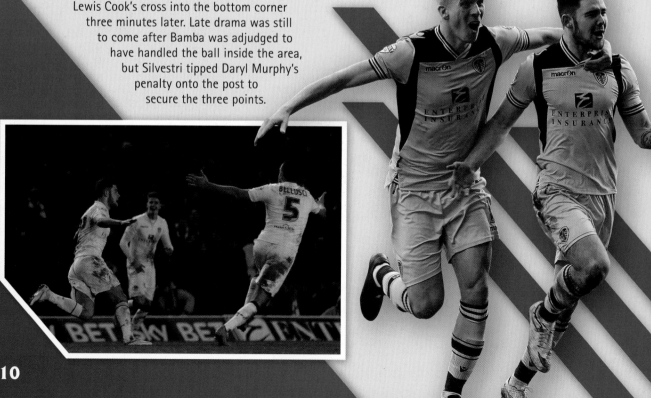

Fulham (a), Championship
18.03.2015 3-0 Win

The midweek visit to Craven Cottage saw United extend their unbeaten run to four games with a 3-0 victory over Fulham that wasn't quite as comfortable as the scoreline suggested. Former Leeds strike duo Ross McCormack and Matt Smith were both out to put one over their old club, but the pair passed up a number of golden opportunities early on as the hosts started strongly. Byram's towering, downwards header opened the scoring against the run of play after 40 minutes, before Bamba and Antenucci added to Leeds' tally in the second half.

Sheffield Wednesday (a), Championship
25.04.2015 2-1 Win

The final away day of the season was one to remember as Leeds came from behind to take the bragging rights over their Yorkshire rivals at Hillsborough. Wednesday had taken the lead after 36 minutes courtesy of a contentious Chris Maguire penalty in front of the travelling fans. But Charlie Taylor tucked away his second goal of the campaign from close range after a scramble inside the area to level things up on 57 minutes. Morison was then sent through on goal in the 72nd minute and, after seeing his initial shot blocked by Keiren Westwood, the striker slotted home to clinch the first win in six games.

Rotherham (h), Championship
02.05.2015 0-0 Draw

2014/15 was brought to a close by an uncharacteristically forgettable Yorkshire derby against Rotherham at Elland Road. Both teams had already secured their Championship statuses and that was evident as the 31,850 inside the ground had little to cheer about on a wet afternoon back in May. The players embarked on a post-match lap of appreciation to thank the fans for their support throughout the campaign, with a number of them, including Aidy White, having played their final game for the club.

Meet the Team

Marco Silvestri

Date of Birth: 02/03/1991

Nationality: Italian

Goalkeeper Marco Silvestri arrived from Serie A side Chievo in summer 2014 and made a big impression at Elland Road during his debut season. He featured 44 times in all competitions as he found himself shortlisted for the Player of the Year award.

Charlie Horton

Date of Birth: 14/09/1994

Nationality: American

USA Under-23 international Charlie Horton was United's first signing in the summer of 2015. The youngster joined from Cardiff City on a free transfer on the recommendation of new goalkeeping coach Richard Hartis, who had worked with the shot-stopper during his time in South Wales.

Ross Turnbull

Date of birth: 04/01/1985
Nationality: English

Former Chelsea and Middlesbrough 'keeper Ross Turnbull added competition for United's number one shirt when he arrived on a free transfer from Barnsley over the summer. Ross, a Champions League winner from his days at Stamford Bridge, has a wealth of experience under his belt and has represented England at Under-19s level.

DEFENDERS

Sam Byram

Date of Birth: 16/09/1993

Nationality: English

Sam Byram progressed through the Leeds Academy to establish himself as a regular fixture in the first team. 2014/15, his third full season with the senior squad, saw the full-back/winger make 39 appearances and score three goals along the way. He was also shortlisted for the Player of the Year award.

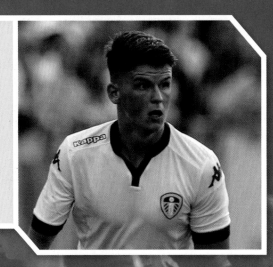

Sol Bamba (Captain)

Date of Birth: 13/01/1985

Nationality: Ivorian

Sol Bamba enjoyed a productive loan spell at Elland Road during the second half of last season. He featured 19 times and occasionally captained the side as United moved to secure his services permanently on a two-year deal from Palermo during the summer.

Liam Cooper

Date of Birth: 30/08/1991

Nationality: English

Summer 2014 signing Liam Cooper was handed the captain's armband for the second half of last season after making a big impression at the heart of the United defence. Cooper ended the campaign with 31 appearances and one goal to his name after finding the back of the net in a home win over Blackpool.

Giuseppe Bellusci

Date of Birth: 21/08/1989

Nationality: Italian

Italian centre-back Giuseppe Bellusci was signed from Catania in summer 2014 as the United squad saw a large number of new arrivals from the continent. Bellusci netted twice during his debut season in England, including a memorable free-kick in the win away to Bournemouth.

Gaetano Berardi

Date of Birth: 21/08/1988

Nationality: Swiss

Gaetano Berardi joined from Sampdoria in July 2014 but endured a testing start to life in England. Two early send-offs meant he was made to wait for a regular run in the team, before the Swiss full-back ended the season strongly down the left of United's defence. He finished 2014/15 with 21 appearances in total.

Charlie Taylor

Date of Birth: 18/09/1993

Nationality: English

Another Academy product, Charlie Taylor, enjoyed a fine 2014/15 campaign after eventually breaking into the side at the start of January. He remained ever-present from there on in and finished the season with two goals – one away to Wolves and one away to Sheffield Wednesday – from his 25 appearances.

Scott Wootton

Date of Birth: 12/09/1991

Nationality: English

Summer 2013 signing Scott Wootton spent part of last season on loan at Championship rivals Rotherham United, but the defender returned to Elland Road and made the right-back spot his own for the second half of the campaign following a string of solid displays.

MIDFIELDERS

Alex Mowatt

Date of Birth: 13/02/1995

Nationality: English

2014/15 Player of the Year Alex Mowatt hit nine goals from 38 appearances last term and earned international recognition with England Under-20s along the way. The Thorp Arch graduate also netted spectacular strikes against Wigan, Wolves and Charlton. Mowatt claimed November 2014's Football League Young Player of the Month award.

Luke Murphy

Date of Birth: 21/10/1989

Nationality: English

Luke Murphy was recalled to the side at the start of 2015 and quickly re-established himself as one of the first names on the team-sheet following a string of impressive midfield performances. His match-winner against Bournemouth was a seasonal highlight from his 32 appearances in total last term.

Lewis Cook

Date of Birth: 03/02/1997

Nationality: English

2014/15 Young Player of the Year Lewis Cook only made his first-team debut as a 17-year-old away to Millwall last season, but the dynamic England youth midfielder soon earned a glowing reputation as one of the country's brightest talents during his 37 appearances. Cook penned a new two-year deal at the club during the summer.

Tommaso Bianchi

Date of Birth: 01/11/1988

Nationality: Italian

Tommaso Bianchi joined from Sassuolo during summer 2014, and the former Italy Under-21s international was a regular fixture in the side for the first half of the season. The midfielder lost his place at the start of 2015 and a knee injury then ruled him out for the remainder of the campaign, limiting him to 24 appearances in total.

Kalvin Phillips

Date of Birth: 02/12/1995

Nationality: English

Kalvin Phillips' impressive displays for United's Under-21s earned the midfielder a first-team debut at Wolves back in April. He maintained his place in the side for the following week's visit of Cardiff and marked it with a goal on his home debut. Phillips signed a new two-year deal at Elland Road in the summer.

Tom Adeyemi

Date of birth: 24/10/1991
Nationality: English

Holding midfielder Tom Adeyemi became United's fifth signing of the summer back in July, joining on a season-long loan deal from Championship rivals Cardiff City. Tom, a product of Norwich City's academy, netted his first goal in Leeds colours during the pre-season friendly defeat to German side Hoffenheim.

Casper Sloth

Date of birth: 26/03/1992

Nationality: Danish

Denmark international Casper Sloth joined United from Superliga side Aarhus in summer 2014. The creative midfielder featured 14 times in total last season after making his debut in the Elland Road win over Bolton Wanderers. Casper is among those players still looking to make an impression at the club after struggling to hold down a regular place in the team.

Stuart Dallas

Date of birth: 19/04/1991

Nationality: Northern Irish

Winger Stuart Dallas became United's seventh new addition of the summer when Uwe Rosler snapped him up from former club Brentford. The Northern Ireland international penned a three-year deal with the option of a fourth at Elland Road after joining for an undisclosed fee. Dallas was among Brentford's stars during last season, and ended his three-year spell at Griffin Park with 76 appearances to his name.

Jordan Botaka

Date of Birth: 24/06/1993

Nationality: Congolese

Highly-rated winger Jordan Botaka arrived on deadline day of the summer 2015 transfer window. Nicknamed 'The Wizard' for his trickery and quick feet, Botaka penned a two-year deal to join from Dutch club Excelsior for an undisclosed fee. The Congo international began his professional career in Belgium with Club Brugge.

Lee Erwin

Date of Birth: 19/03/1994

Nationality: Scottish

Lee Erwin became United's second summer signing of 2015 after penning a three-year contract to move to Elland Road from Motherwell back in June. The young striker, who can also play out wide, had a promising reputation in Scottish football and is now hoping to make his mark in England.

Chris Wood

Date of Birth: 07/12/1991

Nationality: New Zealander

United beat off strong competition to secure the services of Chris Wood on a four-year deal from Leicester City back in July. The New Zealand international striker is a proven goalscorer at Championship level and helped Leicester to promotion in 2014. He also scored the winner against Leeds while on loan at Millwall in 2012.

Mirco Antenucci

Date of Birth: 08/09/1984

Nationality: Italian

Mirco Antenucci joined from Ternana in summer 2014 and the striker ended his debut campaign in English football as United's top goalscorer after finding the net on 10 occasions. He was mainly used as a substitute in the second half of the season, but still made an impact with goals off the bench at Blackpool and Fulham.

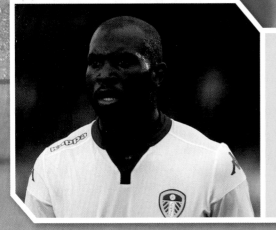

Souleymane Doukara

Date of Birth: 29/09/1991

Nationality: French

Souleymane Doukara was another of summer 2014's arrivals from Italian football, moving to United from Serie B side Catania. He made a bright start to life at Elland Road scoring seven times in his first 15 games. However, the striker found opportunities limited during the second half of the season.

Meet the Head Coach

Becoming the Leeds Head Coach presented Uwe Rosler with what he described as "a great opportunity" when he first took charge at Elland Road back in May. "This is a massive club," the former Brentford and Wigan Athletic boss explained after putting pen to paper on a two-year deal.

Rosler had been without a club for six months having departed Wigan the previous November, but his stellar reputation as a coach in English football, which was built at Brentford and then added to at the DW Stadium, made him an attractive candidate for the United job.

His playing career as a striker spanned over 16 years and included a fruitful four-year spell at Manchester City, where he earned 'hero' status and is still highly regarded after hitting 64 goals in 176 appearances for the Citizens. He actually played against Leeds at Elland Road in 1995, helping City to a 1-0 win. "I remember it buzzing, and being a very intense atmosphere," he recalled. "I think Elland Road should be an absolute fortress."

Prior to joining City, Rosler had resided in German football and he returned there upon his exit from the club, joining FC Kaiserslautern in 1998. A season with Tennis Borussia Berlin followed before he was soon back in England after being snapped up on a free transfer by Southampton. From there the German also had a brief loan spell at West Brom. Sadly for Rosler, his playing days were cut short in 2003 after being diagnosed with lung cancer while at Norwegian side Lillestrom.

But Uwe battled back to a full recovery and returned to the club as manager just two years later after obtaining his coaching badges while in remission. He spent two years at the helm there before going on to join fellow Norwegian outfits Viking and Molde.

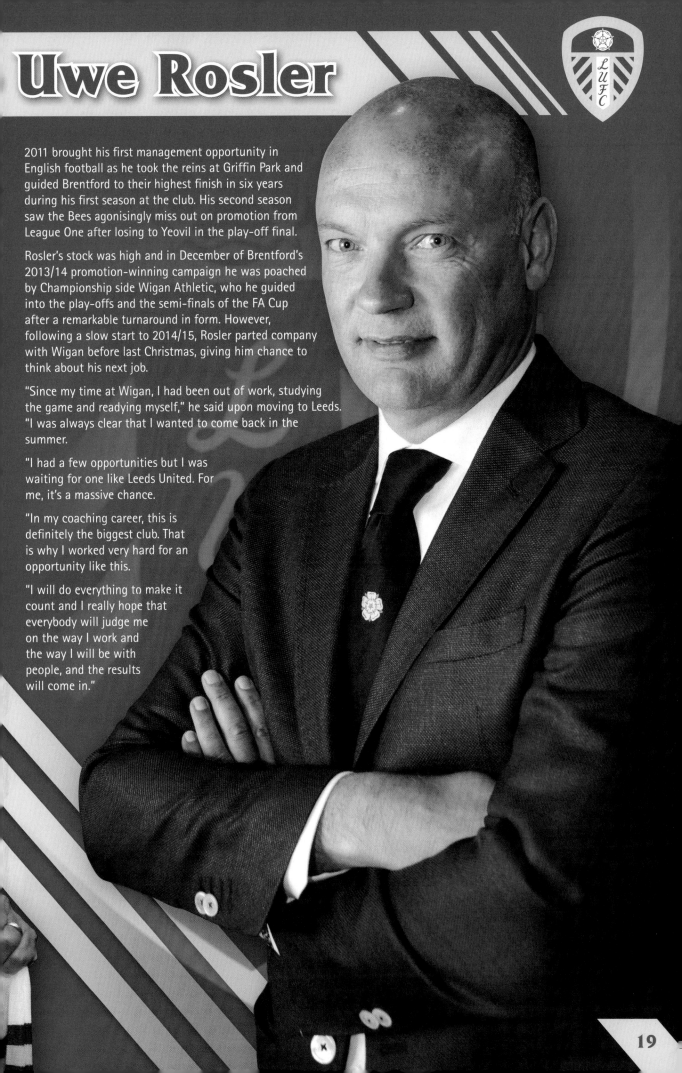

Uwe Rosler

2011 brought his first management opportunity in English football as he took the reins at Griffin Park and guided Brentford to their highest finish in six years during his first season at the club. His second season saw the Bees agonisingly miss out on promotion from League One after losing to Yeovil in the play-off final.

Rosler's stock was high and in December of Brentford's 2013/14 promotion-winning campaign he was poached by Championship side Wigan Athletic, who he guided into the play-offs and the semi-finals of the FA Cup after a remarkable turnaround in form. However, following a slow start to 2014/15, Rosler parted company with Wigan before last Christmas, giving him chance to think about his next job.

"Since my time at Wigan, I had been out of work, studying the game and readying myself," he said upon moving to Leeds. "I was always clear that I wanted to come back in the summer.

"I had a few opportunities but I was waiting for one like Leeds United. For me, it's a massive chance.

"In my coaching career, this is definitely the biggest club. That is why I worked very hard for an opportunity like this.

"I will do everything to make it count and I really hope that everybody will judge me on the way I work and the way I will be with people, and the results will come in."

Meet the backroom staff

The summer brought a string of changes at the club, including a number of key additions to the backroom staff at Thorp Arch. Here we profile those working alongside Head Coach Uwe Rosler.

Rob Kelly
– Assistant Head Coach

Former Leicester City boss Rob Kelly was Uwe Rosler's first new recruit of the summer, arriving just two weeks after the Head Coach was unveiled at Elland Road.

Kelly had previously been in the Premier League with West Brom, where he took caretaker charge following the departure of Alan Irvine at the start of 2015.

He boasts a wealth of experience in the game and represented Leicester, Tranmere Rovers, Wolverhampton Wanderers and Burton Albion during a playing career that was cut short due to injury at the age of just 24.

Kelly spent 15 months in charge of the Foxes, and had caretaker manager spells at Preston North End, Sheffield Wednesday, Nottingham Forest and West Brom, having initially assisted at each club.

He can usually be found putting the players through their paces, going through the coaching drills at Thorp Arch or ahead of kick-off on matchdays, and offering Rosler a second opinion on all first-team matters.

What Uwe said...

"Rob has been in this league for many, many years. He has been in the Premier League.

"He knows the league inside out, and he knows the players inside out. He's good on the training field.

"I was looking to bring in somebody experienced who had worked at this level for quite some time and I think that Rob is a very good option. We have known each other for a while.

"I'm happy to have such an experienced man next to me.

"He's the second man in command. He is influential in the day-to-day running of our team in terms of training sessions."

Julian Darby
– First-team Coach

Julian Darby was appointed as the club's new first-team coach at the start of July, just in time for the players returning for pre-season training.

Darby previously held the same position at Championship rivals Nottingham Forest where he worked alongside Rob Kelly.

The 47-year-old has also coached at Derby County, Bolton Wanderers and Preston North End during his career so far.

His playing days as a midfielder, which were brought to a close upon retirement in 2001, saw Darby represent Bolton, Coventry City, West Brom, Preston, Rotherham United and Carlisle United.

Darby's role is exactly what it says on the tin, and he can be spotted coaching the first-team at Thorp Arch or ahead of kick-off on matchdays.

What Uwe said...

"Rob recommended Julian – they've worked with each other before so there's a very good dynamic between the two.

"There's a lot of energy and a lot of enthusiasm out on the training field – I think that is absolutely needed."

Richard Hartis
– Goalkeeping coach

Goalkeeping coach Richard Hartis came through the door at Elland Road shortly after Kelly's arrival and played a big role in United securing their first signing of the summer.

Hartis, who arrived from Cardiff City, recommended young Bluebirds goalkeeper Charlie Horton to the club from their time working together in South Wales.

Hartis had previously worked in Norway as part of Ole Gunnar Solskjaer's backroom staff at Molde, and held the role of Head of Academy Goalkeeping at Manchester United for the 10 years before that.

He also worked as a goalkeeping coach for England's youth teams.

What Uwe said...

"I'm very happy with Richard Hartis. I know him from Norway, and I also knew him at Man United.

"He has experience and knowledge on the training pitch, and knows about creating that winning environment."

Thorp Arch:
Rising Stars

Young striker Lewis Walters endured a frustrating 2014/15 campaign after picking up a knee injury in pre-season. Lewis, who can also play out wide, looked close to making his first-team breakthrough during summer 2014, but found himself ruled out of action until February after falling awkwardly in a friendly away to Mansfield. He remains highly-rated at Elland Road despite his injury setback, and the Thorp Arch graduate signed a new one-year contract with the club during the summer. Lewis featured 10 times for the Under-21s last term, scoring on three occasions.

Lewis Walters
Born:
28.03.1995
Position:
Striker

Alex Purver
Born:
01.12.1995
Position:
Midfielder

Central midfielder Alex Purver captained the Under-21s for large parts of 2014/15 before his season was sadly cut short due to injury. Alex, who operates just in front of the defence, has previously travelled with the first-team squad on matchdays to give him a taster of things to come. He featured 21 times for the Under-21s during the last campaign, and earned plaudits for his displays alongside Kalvin Phillips in the heart of midfield. Alex signed a new one-year deal at the club over the summer.

Lewie Coyle
Born:
15.10.1995
Position:
Defender

Full-back Lewie Coyle had a nightmare start to 2014/15 after picking up a serious injury in the Under-21s' first pre-season friendly. It ruled him out for the opening months, but Lewie returned to fitness and secured the right-back spot once again with a number of solid displays. The Hull-born defender also signed a new one-year contract during the summer and trains regularly with the first-team.

Tyler Denton
Born: 06.09.1995
Position: Defender

Luke Parkin
Born: 15.08.1995
Position: Striker

Left-back Tyler Denton joined the Leeds United Academy at the age of seven and progressed through the age groups to become the Under-21s' most regular fixture in the side last season, featuring 27 times on the way to an impressive third-place finish. Tyler was another of the youngsters who signed a new one-year deal at Elland Road during the summer.

Striker Luke Parkin also joined the Academy at the age of seven and has worked his way up to become a familiar face in the Under-21s. Last season saw Luke net nine times from 27 appearances, with nine of them as a substitute, and was rewarded with a new one-year deal over the summer. Luke came close to the first-team last season, just missing out on the matchday squad at home to Fulham.

Young professionals

Striker Frank Mulhern (left), goalkeeper Bailey Peacock-Farrell (centre) and midfielder Tom Lyman (right) all signed their first professional contracts with the club over the summer after progressing through the ranks at Thorp Arch.

The trio all featured regularly for the Under-18s last season and are now looking to take the next steps in their careers by pushing towards the first-team at Elland Road.

Mirco Antenucci

Pre-Season Tour: Aust

Uwe Rosler and the United squad prepared for the 2015/16 season by heading out to Austria for a week-long training camp back in July...

DAY ONE:

An early start at Manchester Airport saw the team fly to Munich, where the coach was waiting to take them across the German border to their Austrian base to spend the next week in Kossen. The mountainous surroundings provided a picturesque backdrop, but there was no time for admiring the view as the squad headed straight for the training pitch at the home of FC Kossen. That evening saw the new signings take on their initiations after dinner, and the star of the show was undoubtedly Chris Wood performing New Zealand's traditional Haka routine.

DAY TWO:

The hard work really began on the second day into the tour, with the players put through morning and afternoon training sessions in differing weather conditions. Sweltering temperatures of up to 32 degrees made the morning a real test, until the heavens opened in the afternoon to afford the players something of a cool-down during their second session. Young striker Lewis Walters explained: "It's very hot. Before you even start training, you're sweating. You've got to get a lot of water on board, get hydrated and then enjoy the session."

DAY THREE:

Preparations for the friendly with Eintracht Frankfurt stepped up another level on the Monday morning before the game. Rosler went through his tactics with the players and worked on the team's shape in training. He said: "We've been working on more football specific fitness, around roles and responsibilities for certain positions. We've been working on team shape and more speed orientated exercises." The Head Coach then allowed them the afternoon off to recharge their batteries and many players headed for the nearby lake for a day of relaxation ahead of the tour's opening friendly.

DAY FOUR:

Matchday. A light training session was held in Kossen before the players made the hour-long trip to Eugendorf Sportzentrum, where they would meet Bundesliga side Eintracht Frankfurt. Around 700 Leeds fans were estimated to have made the trip, making for a lively atmosphere in an intimate ground. Steve Morison opened the scoring for United with a well-taken strike in the first half, but Frankfurt hit back after the break through Johannes Flum and Stefan Reinartz to secure the victory. Rosler said: "We got exactly what we hoped for – we played against a team with very good ball possession. We worked very hard against them and we worked extremely well in the shape. The longer the game went on, the more we adapted to their quality a little bit better."

DAY FIVE:

Rosler invited supporters to an open training session in Kossen to see the players who didn't start against Frankfurt being put through their paces. Those who had started the game – all playing at least 60 minutes – remained in the hotel gym for recovery sessions. Another afternoon off followed, and the players were treated to a surprise rafting excursion in Austria's stunning Saalach River. The day was perfect for a team bonding session as five boats of players and coaches set sail, stopping off along the way for jumps into a waterfall. Goalkeeping Coach Richard Hartis said: "It's what pre-season is about. It's about working hard, getting some togetherness and preparing ourselves for the season coming."

DAY SIX:

The penultimate day in Austria saw the players put through a tough training session in the morning before being given another afternoon off to explore the area. The LUTV crew had been working hard all day to put together a video from the rafting afternoon. They played it on the hotel's big screen after dinner, much to the delight of the players who took great joy in re-watching the moment Sol Bamba overcame his fears to jump into the waterfall!

DAY SEVEN:

The players departed Austria after a morning training session, but it wasn't quite home-time as they flew from Salzburg to Oslo to take on more German opposition, Hoffenheim, in another friendly at the Arasen Stadion – home of Lillestrom SK.

The 2015/16 Leeds United home kit has proved to be a big hit with the supporters ever since it was unveiled at Elland Road in the summer.

Here are some of the best photos from the reveal night...

Josh Warrington

Fighting talk – Sam, Alex and Charlie meet local boxer and big Leeds fan Josh Warrington ahead of the new home kit being unveiled.

Q & A

United – ...and takes part in a question and answer session with the Leeds supporters.

Uwe Rosler

United – Head coach Uwe Rosler joins the players on stage...

Home kit reveal

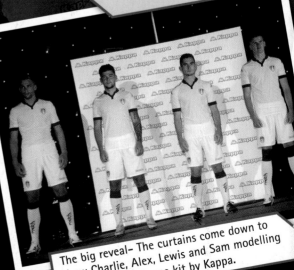

The big reveal– The curtains come down to show Charlie, Alex, Lewis and Sam modelling the 2015/16 home kit by Kappa.

Mowatt and Cook

Young fan

All smiles – Alex and Lewis share a joke on-stage as they pose for photographs in the new kit.

The future – This young fan proudly displays his new Leeds shirt.

On sale

Massimo Cellino

On sale – The shirts were flying off the rails as supporters rushed to be among the first to wear the new Kappa kit.

Proud owner – Leeds president Massimo Cellino couldn't wait to get his hands on the new Kappa shirt.

Best & Worst: Sol Bam

We sat down with defender Sol Bamba to find out his best and worst on a number of different topics...

 Best

 Worst

Moment in football...

 My first professional game with Paris Saint-Germain.

 When we lost the final of the African Cup of Nations with the Ivory Coast.

Away ground you've visited...

 Stamford Bridge, Chelsea.

 Glanford Park, Scunthorpe United.

Car in the Leeds squad...

 My car, a Porsche Cayenne.

 Mine again –it takes up so much petrol!

Person to share a room with...

 Billy Sharp used to be – he was quite funny. He was crazy.

 Souleymane Doukara because he can speak too much when I'd like to sleep!

Dress sense in the squad...

 Mirco is a tidy dresser, he has style.

 There is no worst one!

Music taste in the squad...

👍 Scott Wootton – he puts the music on in the dressing room.

👎 He left us in the summer, Stuart Taylor!

Banter in the squad...

👍 It used to be Sharpy.

👎 Me – I don't joke.

Film you've watched...

👍 Gladiator.

👎 Fifty Shades of Grey!

Country you've visited...

👍 Turkey, my family enjoyed it there.

👎 Congo.

Skills in the squad...

👍 It's between Cookie and Sam Byram.

👎 The goalkeeper, Marco Silvestri!

THE BIG LEEDS UNITED

Put your knowledge to the test and see how much attention you have been paying to these pages so far with our Big Leeds United Quiz.

01 Striker Lee Erwin joined Leeds from which Scottish club over the summer?

02 At which club did goalkeeping coach Richard Hartis and summer signing Charlie Horton previously work together?

03 Midfielder Kalvin Phillips made his Leeds debut away to which club last season?

04 Which of the following clubs did Uwe Rosler NOT represent during his playing career – West Brom, Manchester City or Tottenham Hotspur?

05 Which Leeds legend is our club mascot – the Kop Cat – named after?

06 Striker Chris Wood plays international football for which country?

07 Which Italian club did Leeds sign Sol Bamba from on a permanent deal over the summer?

08 Who is the club's all-time top goalscorer?

09 Who was named the Leeds United Player of the Year for 2014/15?

10 Who was Leeds' top goalscorer in the 2014/15 season?

QUIZ

11 Leeds did the double over which of the following teams last season – Reading, Middlesbrough or Bolton?

12 Can you name the three youngsters who signed their first ever professional contracts with the club during the summer?

13 Which Spanish club did Leeds beat to reach the Champions League semi-finals in 2001?

14 Against which club did Liam Cooper score his first Leeds goal last season?

15 What is Julian Darby's job title as part of the club's backroom staff?

16 There are two statues outside Elland Road stadium. Can you name the Leeds United legends that they are of?

17 Which stand at Elland Road holds the most supporters?

18 What nationality is full-back Gaetano Berardi?

19 How many goals did Sam Byram score in 2014/15?

20 What is the name of Leeds United's training ground?

Answers can be found on page 60 ... but no cheating! Good luck!

Behind the Scenes:

Season Ticket Campaign

On a sunny afternoon back in spring, four Leeds United stars headed for the playing fields overlooking Elland Road to film the 2015/16 Season Ticket campaign video – 'Real History. Real Future. Real Choice.'

Fresh from first-team training at Thorp Arch earlier in the day, Alex Mowatt, Lewis Cook, Sam Byram and Charlie Taylor were challenged to a game by a group of youngsters enjoying their half-term holiday.

Under the watchful eyes of Leeds legends Eddie Gray and Norman Hunter, it proved to be more than just a kick-about as the two sides contested a competitive, free-scoring game. And when local boxer Josh Warrington declared "next goal's the winner" after losing count of the scoreline, it was the underdogs who emerged victorious...

There's only one way to decide who gets the next speaking part –a good old game of 'Rock, paper, scissors'...

The lads assess their opponents for the afternoon. There are some tired legs from the training session that morning, but they are confident of a win. In fact, Alex is that confident he decides to play with his hat on backwards.

It's time for the action to get underway and Charlie, Alex and Sam are in relaxed mood ahead of kick-off. They're a little bit more used to playing in front of the cameras than their opponents...

Lewis has the first speaking part and does his best to keep a straight face while Alex, Sam and Charlie try to put him off. Lewis was out injured at the time of filming, meaning he was forced to watch his team-mates from the sidelines.

Legendary pair Eddie Gray and Norman Hunter cast an eye over proceedings. With over 1,000 Leeds appearances between them, they know a thing or two about what it takes to pull on that famous white shirt.

"Don't even think about putting this on Snapchat, lads," Lewis begs, as Alex and Sam have their phones ready for him to slip up. Thankfully, only a couple of takes are needed and Lewis knows it will soon be their turn in front of the cameras.

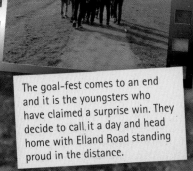

The goal-fest comes to an end and it is the youngsters who have claimed a surprise win. They decide to call it a day and head home with Elland Road standing proud in the distance.

If you haven't already seen the 'Real History. Real Future. Real Choice.' video, head to the Leeds United official YouTube channel to watch it in full.

Insider: Instagram

Former Wigan and Brentford boss Uwe Rosler is unveiled as the club's new head coach.

Lewis Cook is caught on camera by his team-mates during the Season Ticket video filming

Striker Lee Erwin proudly displays his new colours at Elland Road shortly after signing a three-year deal from Scottish side Motherwell

The club's official Instagram account – '@lufcofficial' – brings fans closer to the action with images from behind-the-scenes and in-play at Elland Road, Thorp Arch and beyond. Here are a selection of some of our favourites from the past year...

Young midfielder Kalvin Phillips puts pen to paper on his new two-year contract at Elland Road.

USA Under23 international goalkeeper Charlie Horton meets head coach Uwe Rosler after signing for Leeds.

Lewis Cook signs his new contract with Leeds owner Massimo Cellino

Local boxer Josh Warrington is a huge Leeds fan, and he shows off his latest belt to the Elland Road crowd ahead of kick-off against Blackburn.

The Soccer AM cameras pitch up at Thorp Arch as the lads take on the famous Crossbar Challenge.

The tunnel sees plenty of action and is all set for another busy matchday at Elland Road.

More silverware for Alex Mowatt, who is presented with the Yorkshire Evening Post's Player of the Year award.

Spot the difference

Can you work out the nine changes in this picture of Lewis Cook in training at Thorp Arch?

Turn to page 60 for the solution.

Wordsearch

Can you spot the names of 10 current Leeds players hidden in our wordsearch?

```
R  L  G  Y  H  N  K  K  M  C  N  T
T  L  D  J  H  Y  D  A  G  R  I  L
B  L  Y  R  Z  P  R  G  K  T  R  J
M  E  L  D  M  Y  R  T  Z  H  T  P
S  M  R  T  B  M  Q  U  N  X  S  T
P  R  Z  A  W  L  T  Z  M  E  E  A
I  B  X  W  R  T  C  K  R  F  V  Y
L  M  D  T  A  D  L  W  G  R  L  L
L  L  R  W  H  N  I  L  T  G  I  O
I  T  O  D  H  N  N  M  Z  T  S  R
H  M  C  R  E  P  O  O  C  N  B  P
P  P  B  C  O  O  K  N  N  Z  T  B
```

Find the list of words below:

Silvestri   Erwin
Mowatt   Cooper
Cook   Murphy
Berardi   Phillips
Taylor   Byram

Turn to page 61 for the solution.

41

Made in Leeds:

Homegrown talents

As Thorp Arch continues to produce players ready to slot straight into the first-team at Elland Road, we decided to take a look at some of the Academy's success stories from down the years...

Fabian Delph

Born in Bradford, England midfielder Fabian Delph joined our academy in 2001, and made his first-team debut at Derby in 2007 after being made captain of the reserve side.

But it was the 2008/09 campaign under Gary McAllister, and then Simon Grayson, that he truly made his mark, scoring six times in his 51 appearances on the way to the League One play-off semi-finals. Delph's sensational form was said to have attracted interest from a host of top-flight sides and he made a big-money switch to Aston Villa in summer 2009.

Injuries have hampered his progression somewhat in recent years but, having especially impressed in his appearances for England, Delph has grown into the all-encompassing midfielder most United fans knew he would.

James Milner

The Leeds United Academy's biggest success story since the turn of the millennium is almost certainly James Milner. Now a Liverpool player with two Premier League titles, an FA Cup winner's medal and over 50 England caps to his name, the versatile midfielder's achievements surpass those of any of his former Thorp Arch team-mates.

Having joined the Academy aged 10, Milner soon burst onto the scene, becoming the Premier League's second youngest player at 16 years and 309 days as a substitute in November 2002's 4-3 win at West Ham.

He then went on to become the division's youngest goalscorer at Sunderland on Boxing Day of the same year. Though perhaps his finest moment in a white shirt came two days later, netting a sublime goal in the 2-0 win over Chelsea at Elland Road. Milner made a total of 54 appearances for the Whites before departing for Newcastle in July 2004.

Aaron Lennon

Aaron Lennon's ascent almost mirrored that of Milner, as the Chapeltown-born winger also had Boxing Day joy at Sunderland by netting his first goal for the club in 2004's 3-2 win.

Over a year earlier, Lennon had become the Premier League's youngest player aged 16 years and 129 days as a substitute in August 2003's 2-1 defeat away to his future club Tottenham.

The now 27-year-old made the majority of his 43 United appearances in the Championship, before moving to White Hart Lane in 2005 where he flourished and collected 21 England caps. Last season saw Lennon enjoy a loan spell at fellow Premier League outfit Everton.

Danny Rose

Another Thorp Arch graduate now proving his worth at Spurs is full-back Danny Rose. Rose never appeared for Leeds but his reputation as a youngster saw Martin Jol stump up a reported £1million to secure his services.

It took Rose some time to establish himself in North London before becoming a regular fixture in recent seasons, with loan spells at Watford, Peterborough, Bristol City and Sunderland aiding his development.

Rose is yet to make a senior appearance for England, despite being called up for recent friendlies, but he represented Great Britain at the 2012 Olympics. He was team-mates with Delph at Thorp Arch and the pair have since shared the same training pitch at St George's Park with England.

Jonny Howson

And other notable Academy graduates in recent years:

Alex Mowatt	Dominic Poleon
Sam Byram	Alex Cairns
Lewis Cook	Chris Dawson
Charlie Taylor	Tom Lees
Kalvin Phillips	Ben Parker
Aidy White	

The Champions League

The 2015/16 season marks 15 years since Leeds took the UEFA Champions League by storm and, against the odds, reached the semi-finals after a remarkable campaign in Europe's elite competition.

David O'Leary's exciting young side secured an impressive third-place finish in 1999/2000 to book a spot in the qualifying stages of the following season's Champions League. Entering the competition as underdogs, United were pitted against 1860 Munich of Germany and would need to see them off over two legs, starting at Elland Road, in order to reach the group stages.

A 2-1 victory at home was backed up by a 1-0 win in Germany, and Leeds were in the hat for the first group-stage draw. Barcelona, AC Milan and Besiktas were pulled out as the opposition, with few giving United a chance of anything but an early exit. That looked to be the case when Barcelona stormed to a 4-0 win at the Nou Camp in the opening game. But a 1-0 home victory over Milan, followed by a 6-0 trouncing of Besiktas, gave a major boost to the chances of "O'Leary's babies".

The final three group games all produced draws, meaning Leeds edged into second position one point ahead of Barcelona, thanks to a famous 1-1 tie with Milan in the San Siro courtesy of Dominic Matteo's header. Progression was sealed with an impressive nine points on the board.

Many thought things couldn't get much tougher for Leeds when the second group-stage draw came around. But Real Madrid, Lazio and Anderlecht were picked out of the hat, and the size of the task ahead once again became huge in the face of even more European footballing heavyweights.

Leeds' second group-stage campaign started in a similar vein to their first as Spanish giants Real Madrid proved to be too strong in a 2-0 win. But United went on to win their next three on the trot, starting with an eye-catching victory away to Lazio thanks to Alan Smith's cool finish. Anderlecht were then seen off at Elland Road, with Ian Harte and Lee Bowyer on target in a 2-1 win, before the return game in Belgium brought Leeds' finest display of the tournament so far as they cruised to a stylish 4-1 victory.

With nine points to their name, a 3-2 defeat at the Bernabeu to Real Madrid had little impact and by the time the closing fixture of the second group stage came around, United's progression was already secure. Lazio were the visitors as Elland Road witnessed a thrilling 3-3 draw in an entertaining end to the stage.

Next up were the quarter-finals and the size of the task showed no sign of easing, as reigning Spanish champions Deportivo La Coruna were pulled out of the hat as United's next opponent. But a breathtaking night in West Yorkshire saw O'Leary's side all but seal progression to the semi-finals. "3-0 to the weakest link", were the ironic chants from the Elland Road crowd as goals from Harte, Smith and Rio Ferdinand sealed a stunning victory. Deportivo threatened to make United sweat in the return leg, winning 2-0 in Spain, but Leeds saw it out to book their place in the last four.

Spanish opposition were drawn against Leeds again in the semis, this time in the shape of La Liga giants Valencia. But this was where the European adventure was to come to an end. Neither side were able to break the deadlock in the first leg at Elland Road, but Valencia eased to a 3-0 win in the Mestalla Stadium the following week to book their place in the final against eventual winners Bayern Munich.

Crossword

Turn to page 61 for the solution.

▶ ACROSS

1 Name Uwe Rosler's assistant coach at Elland Road. (3,5)

4 Which nationality is full-back Gaetano Berardi? (5)

6 Liam Cooper plays in this position. (7)

7 Which team did Massimo Cellino own in Italy? (8)

8 Who was the club's first summer signing of 2015? (7,6)

11 From which club did Leeds sign striker Lee Erwin? (10)

12 Name the young midfielder who scored on his home debut last season. (6,8)

13 Sam Byram scored his first goal of last season away to this club. (12)

▼ DOWN

2 Leeds kicked off the 2015/16 Championship season against which team? (7)

3 Who was the club's top goalscorer last season? (5,9)

5 Name the Italian club that Leeds signed Sol Bamba from. (7)

8 Uwe Rosler played for which Manchester club? (4)

9 Which stand at Elland Road is also known as the Kop? (5,5)

10 Who won the 2014/15 Player of the Year award? (4,6)

12 Who makes Leeds United 's kit? (5)

Gaetano Berardi

Player of the Year 2014/15

2014/15 Player of the Year: Alex Mowatt

The Leeds supporters voted Alex Mowatt as the 2014/15 Player of the Year to cap an outstanding second season in the first team at Elland Road. The young midfielder was also recognised by his team-mates in claiming the Players' Player of the Year award after hitting nine goals in 38 appearances last term.

The England youth international pipped fellow nominees Marco Silvestri, Sam Byram, Luke Murphy and Lewis Cook to the main award, as chosen by the fans.

Alex said: "The supporters have been with us home and away so I'd like to thank them for voting for me. The support has been tremendous this season.

"The last two seasons have been a dream really, being in the first team. I'd like to thank the managers and everyone at the Academy.

"All the staff, the physios and the fitness coaches have been a massive part of my career so far."

Young Player of the Year: Lewis Cook

Lewis Cook only made his debut as a substitute on the opening day of 2014/15 and was just 17 at the time, but the talented midfielder wasted no time in making his mark last season. The fans voted in their masses to crown Lewis as the Young Player of the Year and he rewarded their faith just over a week later by signing a new contract at the club.

Did you know?

Lewis was also crowned as the 2015 Championship Apprentice of the Year and was named in FourFourTwo magazine's Top 50 players outside the Premier League.

Goal of the Season: Rodolph Austin

Rodolph Austin – or Rudy as the Leeds fans called him – beat off some stiff competition (see page 52) to collect the Goal of the Season award for his unstoppable, dipping strike against eventual promotion-winners Watford. The Jamaican spotted Heurelho Gomes off-guard and sent a half-volley flying over the helpless goalkeeper's head and into the net in front of Elland Road's South Stand.

The Bobby Collins Unsung Hero: Shaun Ford

The first ever Bobby Collins Unsung Hero award – named after our inspirational captain during the 1960s – was handed to a worthy winner in the shape of Academy kitman Shaun Ford. Shaun plays a key role in making everything tick behind the scenes at Thorp Arch and is a hugely popular figure at the training ground.

Did you know?

Shaun used to pick England star Fabian Delph up from Bradford and give him a lift to training during his early days at Leeds.

Did you know?

For the past six seasons, the Player of the Year winner has also been voted as the Players' Player of the Year. They are Alex Mowatt (2015), Ross McCormack (2014), Sam Byram (2013), Robert Snodgrass (2012), Max Gradel (2011), Patrick Kisnorbo (2010).

Alex Mowatt's...

...dream XI

Leeds United Player of the Year Alex Mowatt picks the ultimate starting line-up from his lifetime...

Formation: 4-3-3

Left Wing:
Cristiano Ronaldo

Striker:
Ronaldo

Right Wing:
Lionel Messi

Centre Midfield:
Andres Iniesta

Centre Attacking Midfield:
Ronaldinho

Centre Midfield:
Zinedine Zidane

Left Back:
Ashley Cole

Centre Back:
John Terry

Centre Back:
Carles Puyol

Right Back:
Philipp Lahm

Goalkeeper:
Manuel Neuer

Sizzling Strikes!

Goals of the Season

Leeds scored exactly 50 Championship goals during the 2014/15 campaign and the fans were spoilt for choice when it came to selecting their top five at the end of the season. Here are the ones that made the shortlist...

Alex Mowatt vs Wigan (a)
Saturday March 7 2015, 51st minute

Alex Mowatt was the man of the moment for large parts of the season and he showed just why with this match-winning strike at Wigan Athletic. The 20-year-old's second-half effort proved to be the difference at the DW Stadium as he took his tally to an impressive eight for the season. Billy Sharp's through ball cannoned back off former United defender Jason Pearce and into the path of the arriving Mowatt, who let fly with his 'weaker' right foot from the edge of the area, leaving Scott Carson helpless as it soared into the net to spark pandemonium among the travelling fans.

Giuseppe Bellusci vs Bournemouth (a)
Tuesday September 16 2014, 82nd minute

Giuseppe Bellusci's breathtaking first goal for the club couldn't have come at a better time. As a tight game entered the final 10 minutes at high-flying Bournemouth's Goldsands Stadium, a moment of magic was needed to separate the two sides with the score level at 1-1. United were awarded an 82nd-minute free-kick around 30 yards from goal and up stepped a confident-looking Bellusci. The Italian duly delivered, too, unleashing a wicked strike into the top corner and beyond the sprawling Lee Camp to put United ahead in spectacular fashion.

Luke Murphy vs Bournemouth (h)
Tuesday January 20 2015, 36th minute

"It had a bit of swerve on it and sometimes they go in, most of the time they end up in Row Z!" remarked a modest Luke Murphy after hitting a stunning winner over Bournemouth back in January. The midfielder made it two goals in as many games with a sweetly-struck, left-footed effort in front of the South Stand to sink the eventual champions. Some smart build-up play down the right freed up Murphy, allowing him to drive forward before sending a swerving strike away from Artur Boruc and into the top corner. It meant United ended a winless run of nine games in all competitions, kick-starting a remarkable turnaround in form on a memorable night at Elland Road.

Rodolph Austin vs Watford (h)
Saturday February 28 2015, 19th minute

Rodolph Austin's unstoppable strike against Watford was a worthy winner of the 2014/15 Goal of the Season award. The midfielder's third goal of the season, and his tenth for the club, was perhaps his finest in United colours despite the eventual outcome. Austin latched onto Sam Byram's knock-down on the corner of the box, took one touch to tee himself up before looping a stunning half-volley over Heurelho Gomes' head during a dream start at Elland Road. Watford managed to turn things around, coming back from two goals down, but Austin's goal remained one of the season's finest pieces of individual brilliance.

Souleymane Doukara vs Blackpool (h)
Saturday November 8 2014, 31st minute

A comprehensive first-half display brought all three United goals in the 3-1 win over Blackpool, including a breathtaking team attempt rounded off calmly by Souleymane Doukara. Byram intercepted a cross inside the United area and began the swift move up-field, with Mirco Antenucci and Adryan exchanging passes before the Brazilian glided forward, unlocking the backpedalling Blackpool defence on his way. Doukara, charging forward, was slotted into the area and calmly tucked it into the bottom corner with the finishing touch the move deserved.

Marco Silvestri

Quiz: Anagrams

Can you re-arrange the words below to work out the names of current Leeds United players?

Hair Color Then

Reel Wine

Late Max Two

Cart Iconic Menu

Samba Lob

Plash Villi Pink

Pure Hulk My

Crowd Hi So

Got them all? Great, now turn to p61 to check your answers.

55

Sam Byram

Stuart Dallas

History: Elland Road

As the song goes, Elland Road has been 'the only place for us' since Leeds United Football Club was founded way back in 1919. With a capacity of 37,890, it is England's 12th largest football ground and the second biggest outside the Premier League.

The ground has previously hosted England international fixtures and FA Cup semi-finals as a neutral venue. It used to be the home of Holbeck Rugby Club, and rugby league side Hunslet Hawks also occupied Elland Road for a period during the 1980s.

Aside from football, the stadium housed the Tri-Nations finals in both 2004 and 2005, and was one of the host venues for the 2015 Rugby World Cup.

And it's not just sporting events that Elland Road can stage, with the likes of Queen, U2, the Happy Mondays, Kaiser Chiefs and Rod Stewart having all played concerts at the home of United.

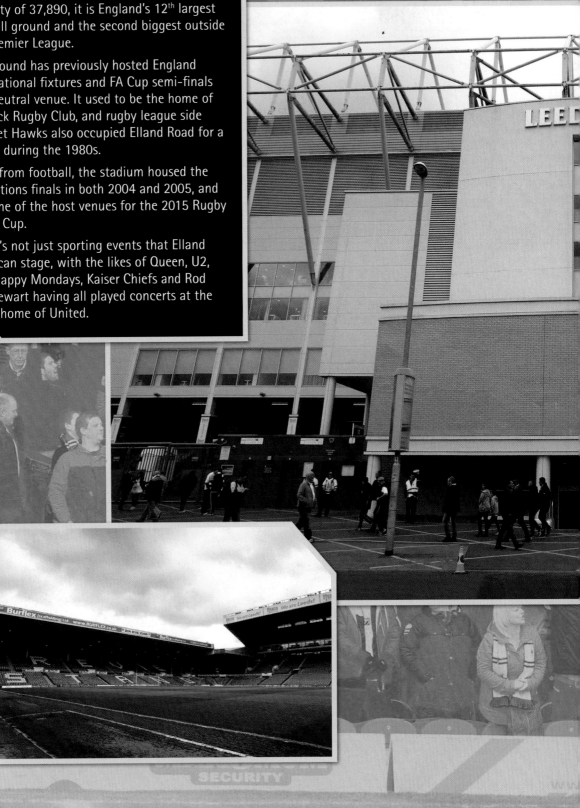

The ground is made up of four main stands, and the highest ever attendance at Elland Road was 57,892 for an FA Cup Fifth Round tie with Sunderland in 1967. More recently, the 40,287 that saw United host Newcastle in 2001 brought Elland Road's biggest attendance of the all-seater era.

The stadium has undergone a series of renovation and upgrade works in recent years, with the most recent being the redevelopment of the East Stand Upper in 2011.

Did you know?

Local rivals Huddersfield Town played two 'home' games at Elland Road during the 1950s after a fire struck their ground. Elland Road was also the home of Bradford City for three games in 1985 after the Bradford Fire Disaster.

Quiz & Puzzle Answers

P34-35 Quiz Answers:

How did you fare in the Big Leeds United Quiz?

1. Motherwell
2. Cardiff City
3. Wolverhampton Wanderers
4. Tottenham Hotspur
5. Lucas Radebe
6. New Zealand
7. Palermo
8. Peter Lorimer
9. Alex Mowatt
10. Mirco Antenucci
11. Middlesbrough
12. Frank Mulhern, Bailey Peacock-Farrell, Tom Lyman
13. Deportivo la Coruna
14. Blackpool
15. First-team coach
16. Billy Bremner and Don Revie
17. East Stand
18. Swiss
19. Three
20. Thorp Arch

Scoreboard:

20/20 Congratulations – that's title-winning form! You're an expert on the world of Leeds United!

18-19 Well done – you're heading for promotion! There isn't much that you don't know about Leeds United!

15-17 Nice work – you've reached the play-offs! A couple of marks short of silverware but an excellent achievement nonetheless!

10-14 Good effort – a top-half finish is something to be proud of! It's a bright start and your knowledge isn't far off the best!

5-9 Unlucky – a bottom-half finish is never the aim! Another read through the Annual is sure to see an improvement, though!

Below 5 Must try harder – you're in danger of relegation! It's time to dig deep and prove you have the knowledge!

P40 Spot the Difference Solution:

P41 Wordsearch Answers:

```
R L G Y H N K K M C N T
T L D J H Y D A G R I L J
B L Y R Z P R G K T R J P
M E L D M Y R T Z H T S P
S M R T B M Q U N X I E T
P R Z A W L T Z M E V A A
I B X W R T C K R F L L Y
L M D T A D L W G R I L L O
L L R W H N I L T G I Y O R
I T O D H N N M Z T S O R
H M C R E P O O C N B P
P P B C O O K N N Z T B
```

Silvestri
Mowatt
Cook
Berardi
Taylor
Erwin
Cooper
Murphy
Phillips
Byram

P46 Crossword Answers:

P55 Anagrams Answers:

Hair Color Then
A: Charlie Horton

Reel Wine
A: Lee Erwin

Late Max Two
A: Alex Mowatt

Cart Iconic Menu
A: Mirco Antenucci

Samba Lob
A: Sol Bamba

Plash Villi Pink
A: Kalvin Phillips

Pure Hulk My
A: Luke Murphy

Crowd Hi So
A: Chris Wood

Where's Lucas?

Can you spot the Kop Cat hiding in the Elland Road crowd?